That morning, Noah was walking in the hills. Suddenly a blinding light lit the sky, and Noah heard God speaking to him.

'I am sending a great flood to the earth,' said God. 'It will destroy everyone, because they are too wicked to live any longer. But I don't want you and your family to die, so you must build an enormous ark. If you all get into the ark before the flood comes, you won't drown.'

God explained exactly how the ark should be built. He gave Noah all the measurements, told him what sort of wood to use, and how to make it watertight.

Noah was amazed. He thought, at first, that the ark sounded rather large for just him and his family, but God told him why it had to be so big. 'I can't save *all* the animals from the flood, but I can make sure that enough survive to start again afterwards,' said God. 'You'll have to collect a male and a female of every kind and take them on board the ark as well. You'll need to pack plenty of food and water for them, as well as for your family. I'll warn you when the flood is about to start, but you'd better start building the ark now.'

and the ARK

illustrated by Leon Baxter
adapted by Belinda Hollyer

Macdonald

There was once a man called Noah, who was wise and kind, and honest in all he did. Noah and his wife had three sons, called Shem, Ham and Japheth. The young men loved their father very much, and tried to be just like him.

God knew that Noah was a good man. When God looked at Noah's family he was pleased, and enjoyed knowing that he had made such people. But it was a different story when God looked at the rest of the world. All the other people spent their time fighting and killing. When they weren't fighting, they were busy stealing. They weren't even kind to their animals. When God saw how these wicked people lived he was sorry that he had ever made them.

'This is dreadful,' thought God. 'I can't bear to watch these evil people. They don't deserve to live.' And so he decided to destroy them all.

If Noah had not been such a good person, God would have destroyed him too. But that seemed unfair, and so God thought of a plan to save him. The next day God explained his plan to Noah.

Noah rushed home to tell his family what God had said. They knew they would have to work quickly to get everything ready, and so they started work that very day.

It was hard to build the ark exactly as God had said, but Noah and his family followed the instructions carefully. They collected all the wood and reeds they needed, and boiled up great cauldrons of pitch to line the walls. Some of the family worked on the ark, while the others gathered food and began to round up the animals.

For months they worked all day, and late into the night. It took weeks of searching to find the animals, and it was even harder to get them back to the ark. But at last the animals, a male and female of every kind, had been collected.

Noah's neighbours came to stare, and stayed to shout rude things. 'What nonsense!' they laughed when they heard about the flood. 'You must be mad – there won't be a flood!'

But Noah and his family kept working. At last the ark was ready, the stores were packed, and the animals had been counted for the last time.

'Well done, Noah,' said God. 'You've finished just in time, for I shall start the flood in seven days. It will rain for forty days and forty nights, and everything will be covered in water. You'd better start loading up now; it will take a week to do it!'

So they did. They loaded the food and water first, storing the containers in the hold. Then they led the animals on board, two by two, and made them all as comfortable as possible.

On the seventh day everything was ready, and the family met by the gangplank. The sky was filled with black clouds, and a cold wind was blowing. A few spots of rain splattered on the roof of the ark, high above them.

'Right,' said Noah, 'we'd better get on board ourselves.' So up they went, two by two: Shem and his wife, Ham and his wife, Japheth and his wife, and last of all Noah and *his* wife. Noah took one last look at the only world he had ever known, sighed, and turned away. He didn't know what was going to happen, but he trusted God, and that would have to do.

As God closed the hatch of the ark behind them, the family heard the rain grow heavier. The flood had begun.

The rain poured down in torrents. At first the lakes and rivers swelled with the extra water. Then, as the rain continued, they broke their banks and flooded across the land to join the seas. The water rose steadily day by day, and soon Noah and his family felt the ark lift from the ground and rock with the waves. Then it was swept away by fierce currents.

It rained for forty days and forty nights, just as God had said. Soon nothing but water could be seen from the window. But there was plenty to do on board, and no time for worrying.

The animals had to be fed and watered, and their compartments needed to be kept clean. When that was done, the family took turns to walk the animals round the lower decks, two by two, so they could stretch their legs. And all the time everyone watched the walls of the ark, in case water leaked in.

Sometimes, late at night, Noah and his wife talked alone. They wondered what the world would be like when the flood stopped, and where the ark would end up. But they knew there was no point in getting anxious, they would just have to wait and see.

One morning Noah woke very early, and wondered why it seemed so quiet. Then he realised that the noise of the rain on the roof had stopped. The flood was over!

Noah ran to the window and peered out. The sky was clear and the water was calm, but still it stretched as far as he could see. Now they would have to wait for the water to go down.

It was much harder waiting for the water to go down than it had been waiting for the rain to stop. God had not told them how long this part would take, so they could only guess. The animals grew restless, and Noah's sons checked the food to see how long it would last. And the ark drifted on and on, across the quiet seas.

At last it stopped moving. Noah realised it was wedged in some kind of rock, although luckily no damage had been done. Each day, he noticed that the level of water on the side of the ark went down a little. 'We must be resting on a mountain peak,' thought Noah, and sure enough other peaks began to show above the water. Everyone felt more cheerful, and even the animals became excited.

Noah began to wonder if there was dry land beyond the horizon. If there was, the flood would probably dry up soon and it would be safe to leave the ark. So he took one of the doves from its cage, and let it fly out of the window. 'She can fly further than my eyes can see,' he thought. 'Perhaps she will bring back hope of dry land.' But the dove returned that evening, tired and wet. She had found nothing.

Noah did not despair. 'I still trust God,' he thought. 'He said he would save us, and he will. I'll try again soon.' So a week later he sent the dove out again. Then he waited at the window, watching the sky and the water. Just before nightfall, the dove returned, fluttering wearily – but in her beak she carried a fresh green twig from an olive tree.

'Look!' cried Noah joyfully. 'She's found a growing tree! I *knew* there must be dry land out there!' And a week later he sent the dove again. This time she did not come back. Noah knew she had found enough dry land to live on. The world was safe again.

The next morning Noah and his family lifted the hatch from the ark, and stepped outside. Then they gasped with delight – for there was dry land all around them. The flood water had gone!

The land looked wonderful. It smelled fresh and clean, and tiny plants were springing up from the soil wherever they looked. The family were so happy they danced and sang, and laughed with pleasure and relief. Their long adventure was over.

But first, they had to let the animals out of the ark. So they put down the gangplank, and ran to open the compartments and arrange the ramps and gates, so the animals could walk out safely. When everything was ready, the family lined up to say goodbye to the animals.

'Come on then, all of you!' called Noah. 'It's safe and dry now, and you can go off and find yourselves new homes.'

So down came the animals, two by two, as happy as Noah's family in the sunshine and fresh air. The family hugged them all as they left, for they had become very fond of them. Then they had breakfast on the mountainside, and began to unpack their belongings.

That day, God spoke to Noah for the last time. 'You and your family have done well,' he said, 'and now I will make a promise to you, and your children, and your children's children. I promise I will never send a flood to destroy everyone again.'

Noah and his family were very pleased at this, for they felt very sorry that so many people had died, even though they had been so wicked. And then God explained how people in the future would know about his promise.

'I will make a sign in the sky,' he said. 'Whenever storm clouds gather and heavy rain falls, I will put a rainbow in the sky. Then people will know that I have remembered my promise. It will rain again in the future, but there will never be another flood like this one.'

This story has been told in many different ways for more than three thousand years. It was first written down in a language called Hebrew. Since then, it has been re-told in almost every language used in the world today.

You can find the story of Noah and the Ark in the Bible. It is in the Book of Genesis, Chapter 6.